£ 1·75

Contents

Published in Great Britain by Stafford Pemberton Publishing Co. Ltd.,
The Ruskin Chambers, Drury Lane, Knutsford, Cheshire WA16 6HA
Printed and bound in Italy
ISBN 0 86030 203 2

Stafford Pemberton Publishing

The SMURFS annual 1980

The Smurfs Meet a Baby Duckling

Do you know the land of the Smurfs? It is a long way from here over many mountains and situated in the middle of a huge forest. There you will find a village with houses that are all in the shape of mushrooms. The Smurfs are very small creatures, they have a blue skin and wear white trousers and a white hat. They have a leader who is called Papa Smurf. Papa Smurf is the oldest Smurf and is very wise. He organises village life and helps all the Smurfs with any problems they might have. Unlike the other Smurfs, he is dressed in red and has a white beard, although he is sometimes very fierce, all the Smurfs love him and respect him.

Life in the Smurf village on the whole is happy. There is always plenty of food to go round and apart from minor disputes, all the Smurfs work happily together.

Although all the Smurfs look alike, they each have their own special character. There is Greedy Smurf, who loves big cream cakes, sweets, jellies, pies in fact any food. Even when he has just finished a big meal and he is really full, he will eat something else if offered.

There is Vanity Smurf, who spends most of his life looking in the mirror and telling himself how much more beautiful he is in comparison to the other Smurfs. There is Brainy Smurf, who wears glasses and is always telling the other Smurfs what to do because he thinks he is so much more clever than they are. There is Naughty Smurf, who is always playing tricks on everyone when they least expect it.

There is Musician Smurf, who is always playing his trumpet and other instruments very badly and there is Grumpy Smurf, who does not like anything or anyone and who always wears a scowl on his face.

These are only a few of the Smurfs because there are 100 Smurfs in all! Smurfs that all look the same, but that all have their own special characteristics. We would like to tell you about them all, but it would take far too long to tell you about all of them and you would be far too bored!

One day, Greedy Smurf and Brainy Smurf were chosen by Papa Smurf to go out searching for nuts in the forest to increase the level of food in the Smurf Stores, which at that time was very low. It was a lovely day, the sun was shining and the birds were singing and the two Smurfs were enjoying being out in the fresh air. Greedy Smurf was singing and even managing to ignore

Brainy's chatter. They had collected quite a few nuts when suddenly Brainy Smurf stopped in his tracks and his mouth dropped open.

"Look what I've found," he called to Greedy Smurf. Greedy Smurf came running over and stared at the strange object that Brainy Smurf was pointing at. It was something tied up in a checked tablecloth. What on earth could it be? They looked again, now the package had started to move! Was there something alive in there? If so, would it be friendly or could it be poisonous? There was no knowing. The Smurfs' brains raced ahead, thinking of all the possibilities.

The Smurfs froze, what should they do? They were both scared, but after a time and many deep breaths, curiosity finally overcame them. Slowly they crept forward and with shaking hands they opened the package . . . .

To their immense surprise the package contained a baby duck who was looking very lost and very forlorn.

"How did this little duckling come to be lost in the middle of the forest?" Asked Greedy Smurf. "And what are we going to do now?"

"We must take him back to his Mother," said Brainy Smurf.

"You should always return lost ducklings to their Mothers, besides Papa Smurf always says . . . ."

"But", interrupted Greedy Smurf. "Where is its Mother? How on earth are we going to find her in this big forest, she could be anywhere. You really say some stupid things."

"What!" Exclaimed Brainy Smurf. "How can you say that, I never say silly things, everybody admires my intelligence and besides, Papa Smurf always agrees with me and. . . . ."

"That's not true!" Cried Greedy Smurf. "You talk too much and you're nothing but an idiot!"

And so the two Smurfs started to argue, they were getting more upset minute by minute and they had completely forgotten about the little duckling.

Upset by all the quarrelling, the baby duck started to cry. The two Smurfs were so astonished, they stopped their arguing.

"Well, I think the best thing we can do is take him home with us," said Brainy Smurf.

"Yes, you're right," agreed Greedy Smurf.

In complete agreement at long last, the trio set off to make their way back to the village. It took a long time, as the duckling was very slow and took two steps to the Smurfs' one.

At last the two Smurfs and the duckling arrived at the Smurf village. All the Smurfs in the village stopped what they were doing and looked in amazement as the trio walked into the village.

"We found the duckling in the forest – his mother was nowhere to be found, so we decided to bring him back to our village," said Brainy Smurf to everyone.

"And I'm going to give him a little piece of my chocolate cake," said Greedy Smurf. At this all the Smurfs were really

surprised, Greedy Smurf never gave anyone any food. "He is almost as good looking as me!" Exclaimed Vanity Smurf.

"And I'm going to play him a happy tune on my trumpet," said Musician Smurf.

"I promise not to play any tricks on him," said Naughty Smurf with a great sigh, it really was hard for him to say that.

Black Smurf said nothing, because he was not in the village at that time.

"The first thing we must do is to find the mother of this little duckling," said Papa Smurf commandingly.

"She must be really concerned about what has happened to her little son."

"You see, you see! I told you so!" Shouted Brainy Smurf, but nobody was listening to him, as all the Smurfs were crowding round the little duckling and admiring him.

After a while the little duckling became bored being admired and began to walk around the village, looking at all objects inquisitively as he went. He looked inside all the little houses and made funny little noises as he discovered something new. Greedy Smurf became very worried that the duckling would knock over his carefully guarded store of nuts, but the only accident that happened was that the duckling tripped over Musician Smurf's trumpet and cracked it. All the other Smurfs couldn't conceal their glee. At long last they would be free of

having to listen to Musician Smurf's bad trumpet playing. But it was not to be, Musician Smurf happily reminded them that he still had his french horn.

Suddenly the little duckling spotted the Smurfs' pond. He hurried towards it, as fast as his little legs would carry him and started to swim. The Smurfs watched fearfully from the edge of the pond, worried that the little duck might drown, but Papa Smurf reassured them that ducks were able to swim from birth.

Grumpy Smurf, who never had much to say, said "Oh good, because I never like to be worried."

Just at that moment Papa Smurf had a brainwave, "There is one sure way of returning this duckling to his Mother, we must inform the storks!"

In fact in the area round where the Smurfs lived, the storks had the important task of bringing the newly born to their animal parents. It had suddenly occurred to Papa Smurf that the duckling must have been lost by a stork passing over the forest on the way to the little duck's Mother. Quickly he asked for volunteers to go and let the storks know that the baby duck had been safely found. Out of almost a hundred volunteers Papa Smurf chose Greedy and Brainy Smurf as they had been the ones to find the duckling in the first place.

Brainy Smurf and Greedy Smurf had a big meal before they left, because they knew they had a long journey ahead of them. At last they were ready and set off on their way to find the place where the storks lived. The journey seemed endless, first through their forest, across fields and country roads and the incessant arguing between the two Smurfs just made it worse. Greedy Smurf kept on stopping and eating the wild food they found on the journey and Brainy Smurf was always trying to impress Greedy Smurf with his knowledge of different subjects.

Finally, just when they thought they could not go any further, they arrived at the storks' nest, which was situated on top of a big chimney on an old country farm.

"We've found it at last," said Brainy Smurf with relief.

Just as the two Smurfs approached the nest they heard one of the storks relating a sorry tale. (The Smurfs were clever creatures that could understand all animal languages).

"Oh dear, oh dear," said the stork. "I'm getting so old these days, I can't see very well and while I was flying over the forest to take a newly born duckling to his mother, the parcel fell out of my beak. I flew for hours and hours over the forest searching for the little duck, but I couldn't find him anywhere. Oh dear, oh dear, oh dear."

It was at this point that Greedy Smurf piped up.

"Excuse me, but we've found your baby duckling." The stork was so happy that she began to clack her beak in joy. The two Smurfs felt very pleased with themselves and said they were only happy to be of assistance.

But, no time was to be wasted, the stork quickly lifted the two Smurfs onto her back and they guided her back to the Smurf village. There she picked up the duckling, who was still swimming happily on the pond. He was in fact thoroughly enjoying himself. She wrapped him up tightly in the tablecloth and off they set again.

Greedy Smurf and Brainy Smurf were to go with the stork so that they would be there to help the duckling with his first

meeting with his Mother and Father. They were also to keep an eye on the stork to make sure that she didn't drop her bundle again! The Smurfs got on the stork's back, she picked up the duckling and then flew over the forest and then higher up into the mountains.

They came eventually to the edge of a sea where a mother duck was pacing up and down, and who was very upset that the son she was expecting had not arrived. She cried out joyfully when she saw the stork arriving and she rushed to take her child under her wing.

When she heard how the Smurfs had found her son and looked after him, she thanked them over and over again and promised to visit them when the duckling could fly.

Picture to colour

WHAT'S WRONG?

The two pictures may look the same but how many differences can you find?

Answer: 10

The Smurfs and the Toys

One cold, December day when the snow lay thick on the ground, two Smurfs were out collecting firewood in the forest as the Smurf village was getting very low on supplies. They were trying to hurry because it was very cold and their feet were already like blocks of ice. Suddenly one of the Smurfs looked round and his mouth dropped open.

"Hey look there is a fly . . . flying reindeer!" He shouted to his friend.

The Smurfs looked at the sky in amazement as the huge, majestic reindeer came swiftly towards them. "Surely he is not coming to see us," said one Smurf to the other. But the Reindeer was, and with a few mighty bounds he landed in front of them.

"Are you the Smurf creatures?" He asked in a deep but gentle voice.

"Yes," replied the two Smurfs who were now holding hands and trembling with fear.

"Good, I've found you at last," replied the Reindeer.

"Can you take me to your leader, Papa Smurf?"

"Yes of course sir," replied the two Smurfs in unison and off they set to lead the Reindeer to their village.

A short time later, with the two Smurfs leading him, the Reindeer entered the Smurf village. All the Smurfs were astonished, they couldn't believe their eyes. Papa Smurf, however, took it all in his stride and he stepped boldly forward and said, "Good day to you Mr Reindeer."

"Good day, Papa Smurf," said the Reindeer "I am one of the reindeers of Father Christmas. He has sent me to ask for your help because he has a serious problem back home and we need some helpers. Quickly, all of you, there is not a moment to waste,

jump on my back and I will take you speedily there."

"Oh well, if it is a crisis, of course we will come, Father Christmas is a dear friend," exclaimed Papa Smurf "Come on Smurfs, hurry up", he called to them all.

It took a while to get everyone on the Reindeer's back and they just thought they were ready when they discovered Vanity Smurf was missing. He was still looking at himself in the mirror in his little house. Papa Smurf dragged him out and at last all was ready and the Reindeer soared gracefully into the sky.

All the Smurfs were very excited, it was the first time they had ever ridden on a reindeer's back, let alone one of *Father Christmas's* reindeer. Because there were so many of them some Smurfs had to sit on the antlers. It was rather scaring, so everybody clung on tightly as the Reindeer galloped through the clouds. They passed over many different fields and lakes and mountains and all the Smurfs marvelled at the glorious scenery that befell them.

Eventually after a long and tiring journey the Reindeer began

to slow down and descend from the sky. Into view came a lovely old cottage situated in a glorious garden full of the most exotic flowers and plants. Rare butterflies and other unusual creatures lived in the garden.

As they got closer they saw a figure standing in the doorway of the cottage – it was Father Christmas and this was his toy workshop. But something was wrong with Father Christmas, his right arm was in a sling!

"Oh, my good friends, how kind of you to come," said Father Christmas as he invited all the Smurfs into his workshop. He began to tell them his tale of woe.

"It was first thing this morning, I was rushing to get everything finished and I slipped on the staircase and broke my arm."

"What bad luck Father Christmas," said Papa Smurf. "Are you very badly hurt?"

"No, not too bad thank you Papa Smurf, but my biggest problem is that I cannot continue making the toys that the children want and it is already 23rd December! Christmas will be here in two days!"

"Don't worry Father Christmas, we are here now, we will finish all your toys for you. Come on Smurfs let's get busy!"

"Oh good, I will go and look after all those lovely sweets," said Greedy Smurf licking his lips.

"I will do all the painting," said Vanity Smurf.

"I think I will go and make the trumpets and drums," said Musician Smurf.

"I'll just go and look at the dolls' beds and make sure they are comfortable enough," said Lazy Smurf.

Papa Smurf, as usual, was the main organiser. He first went and had a long discussion with Father Christmas to find out all the things to do. He finally emerged after quite a long time with an enormous sheet of paper with numerous instructions on it. By this time the Smurfs were getting very agitated as they knew that every second counted.

They all lined up in front of Papa Smurf and he sent them off to do their special tasks. They scurried off in all directions –

Father Christmas's workshop was now a place of frenzied activity. Smurfs were running everywhere. There were several collisions and arguments as they bumped into and tripped over each other. There were so many things to be done: teddybears that needed arms, legs or ears sewed on; toy soldiers that needed a final coat of paint to make them look bright and shiny; puppets that needed all their strings fastened on.

There were so many things to do!

The Smurfs who were best at sewing were hurriedly finishing off all the dolls' clothes.

The mechanical Smurfs were busy fitting wheels to cars.

Other Smurfs were blowing up numerous balloons.

When night came Father Christmas checked the master list with Papa Smurf. There were still many things to be done.

"It's no good Papa Smurf," he said sadly shaking his head. "We are never going to finish."

"Of course we will!" Exclaimed Papa Smurf. "We will work all night, won't we Smurfs?"

"Yes, of course," came the reply, but it seemed to be rather lacking in enthusiasm. They were all getting very tired.

And so the Smurfs carried on painting, cutting, sewing and gluing all night, forcing their tired arms to keep moving and trying to keep their drooping eyelids open. All they wanted to do was to go to sleep, but they knew they could not let Father Christmas down. When dawn came on 24th December all the Smurfs cried out in anguish.

"We cannot do any more work Papa Smurf."

"You must try," encouraged Papa Smurf. "If you give up

now, hundreds of young children will not receive their presents tonight and they will be so disappointed."

These words had their desired effect and the Smurfs with renewed enthusiasm, began to work furiously at their tasks.

"Come on, hurry up, let's go," they all called to each other.

"Hey, be careful! You have stuck that moustache on that lovely little blonde doll," shouted one Smurf to another. Arguments were still going on.

"Give that paint to me," said one Smurf.

"No, I'm using it," replied another.

"OK, that toy is finished, let's wrap it up!"

The hours quickly passed. Would the Smurfs be able to finish in time?

Father Christmas was anxiously watching the grandfather clock – if only he could turn it back a few hours. Suddenly he cried out.

"It's 11 o'clock Papa Smurf, we have less than an hour left."

"Everything will be finished Father Christmas, we have just a few presents to wrap, go and quickly harness your reindeer!"

Meanwhile the Smurfs wrapped up all the last presents in their pretty paper and fastened all the colourful ribbons into bows.

As soon as some Smurfs had finished wrapping a present, others would quickly take it and put it in Father Christmas's sledge.

That night on the stroke of midnight Father Christmas could be seen, as he was every year, driving his reindeer through the sky, stopping every few minutes to deliver his presents. Father Christmas was really happy, nearly as happy as the children would be on Christmas morning as they unwrapped their gifts.

And what about the Smurfs? Would they get any reward for all their help? Well, Father Christmas could not give them any surprises that Christmas, but he assured them that next year they would receive the best presents ever!

Flower Power

The Smurfs and the Windmill

Once upon a time, in a country far from here, there was a windmill situated right in the middle of a vast, rolling plain. The windmill turned all day long and people came from miles around with sacks of grain which was soon converted into freshly ground flour.

The miller, who was called Frank, was respected and loved throughout the land for his honesty and good humour. One busy day the wicked sorcerer Gargamel came to visit him.

"Listen to me miller," said Gargamel "I have got a proposition for you. I have invented a special powder which when added to flour makes it heavier. Half a sack of flour, plus a pinch of my powder, weighs as much as a whole sack full of ordinary flour. This way you can keep half the flour for yourself and we will share the profits."

The miller became very angry and went very red in the face when he heard this dishonest plan and he chased Gargamel away.

As he ran off Gargamel cried, "all right, if that's the way you want it miller, but let me warn you, you have not heard the last of this." The miller just shook his fist at Gargamel and ignored his remarks.

That night, when everybody was fast asleep in their beds, a shadowy figure and a strange looking cat could be seen creeping up to the windmill. The figure checked around the windmill

carefully, laughing evilly to himself. All was quiet and quickly the figure began painting a magic symbol in bright red on the side of the windmill, muttering strange words as he did so. At that moment the moon appeared from behind the clouds and revealed the shadowy person to be Gargamel!

What evil spell was he putting on the windmill? Laughing to himself Gargamel crept stealthily away.

The next day the Smurfs made their way to the windmill. They were all good friends of Frank the miller and had known him a long time. They were off on one of their regular trips to the windmill with their sacks of grain which they wanted made into flour. They then kept the flour with the food in their big Smurf stores. As they went along they sang a Smurfing song and generally they all felt happy.

It was a spring day and the weather was warm and all the Smurfs chatted happily to one another. All that is except Grumpy

Smurf, who was just scowling. He didn't like carrying a sack of grain and he was letting Papa Smurf know!

Papa Smurf however, smiled to himself, he knew all his Smurfs so well. They all had their different ways, but they were good and willing workers and he was very fond of all of them

It did not take the Smurfs long to reach the windmill and they walked up to it still singing happily.

But as soon as they reached the windmill they stopped singing abruptly. Sitting by his door, Frank the miller was looking really worried. He was so deep in thought he did not even notice the Smurfs for a moment.

"What ever is the matter," asked Papa Smurf and all the Smurfs crowded round anxiously.

"Somebody must have put a curse on me," explained the unhappy man. He pointed to a sign on the wall of his windmill

and said "I woke up this morning and discovered that someone must have come in the night and painted that sign on the wall. Since then everything has gone wrong in the windmill. Oh, what am I to do." He let out a big sigh and put his head between his hands.

"What exactly has happened this morning," enquired Papa Smurf.

"Come inside and have a look," replied the upset miller.

Papa Smurf and all the other Smurfs followed Frank inside the windmill. The miller took a big sack of grain and poured it into the thresher.

It is here that the grain passes through the grinding stones, goes down to a lower level and comes out as ground flour. The amount of flour that comes out should be the same weight as the grain that was put in. When the miller checked on the flour, there was only a few handfuls instead of a full sack.

"You see," said Frank the

miller to the Smurfs. "The grain just disappears into thin air once it goes between the grinding stones and I only get about one tenth of what I have put in."

"But isn't there some kind of hole where the grain is escaping?" asked Papa Smurf.

"No, no, I have checked thoroughly myself. Oh dear, what am I going to do? Many people have left their sacks of grain with me and tomorrow they are coming to collect their flour. I can't explain to them what has happened. They won't understand and will only think that I have stolen their flour . . . Nobody will ever come to my windmill again and I will be branded a thief." Frank the miller looked as though he was about to burst into tears, he was so upset.

All the Smurfs looked at Papa Smurf, surely he must have an idea. Papa Smurf's brain was working furiously – there must be an answer he thought.

"Wait a minute, I think I've got it," cried Papa Smurf.

"We will try and remove that magic sign that has bewitched your windmill. Quickly Smurfs," he called. "Go and get some steps and everything we need to try and remove this paint."

The Smurfs scuttled all over the place finding the materials they needed. They all worked furiously at the paint to try and remove it. But whatever they did, it remained as bright as ever.

"Well, that's no good," said Papa Smurf after all their efforts had been in vain. It must be magic paint and nothing can remove the curse from the windmill, unless . . ." Papa Smurf broke out in a smile, he had another idea. He called all the Smurfs to his side and explained how they could help the miller.

"Listen," he said to the miller. "We are going to try an experiment. I can't promise that it will be a success, but it is certainly worth taking a risk."

"Oh please," said the miller. "If you can help me in any way at all, I will do anything for you. I will give you free flour for all time. But please hurry, time is so precious."

The Smurfs soon got to work following the instruction of Papa Smurf. They jumped in amongst the wooden cogs, banging at them with hammers. They oiled all the parts they were told to oil. They polished and sawed. At last, after a few hours work, it was all finished to Papa Smurf's satisfaction. He gave a final check making sure that it was as perfect as it could be.

Papa Smurf was completely satisfied and he said to Frank, "Now you can try and mill a new sack of grain."

"But won't it disappear like all the rest?" he asked anxiously.

"Just put the bag of grain through the thresher and wait and see," said Papa Smurf, smiling to himself.

Papa Smurf was supremely confident, after all, how many times had he ever been proved wrong? Well, not many.

Frank the miller put a large 40lb sack of grain into the thresher and then he went down to collect the flour. For a moment he didn't dare look, but when he did, oh, he was so pleased. It was full to the brim with freshly milled flour and he got another sack, then another and another . . . The Smurfs began to laugh and cheer, Papa Smurf's plan had worked!

"It is quite simple," explained Papa Smurf, after the miller had filled 20 sacks of flour from just a single sack of grain. "The curse on your windmill turned one sack of grain into just a tiny amount of flour. All we had to do was to modify the mechanism of the windmill to make it turn the other way. The curse was then reversed and you can now get several sacks of flour from just one sack of grain.

"Oh, thank you, thank you," said Frank, overwhelmed at what the Smurfs had done for him. "The village folk can come tomorrow and I will have more than enough flour for them."

And who got a nasty surprise the next day? It was Gargamel who came to the windmill to laugh at the miller and to enjoy his downfall. As he arrived at the mill, he couldn't believe his eyes – a crowd of village folk were going away happily with more full bags of flour than usual.

Gargamel was so annoyed at all the smiling faces, especially the miller's, that he kicked himself in disgust.

"What ever has happened!" He babbled.

"I must see what has been going on."

The Smurfs saw him creeping up to the mill.

"Hey look," they cried. "It's the sorcerer Gargamel, I bet he was responsible for the curse on the mill, let's catch him."

Just as Gargamel was walking towards the miller to ask him what happened a huge sack of grain was emptied on his head.

Gargamel was furious, he was gasping, coughing, spitting, all at the same time. He shook his fist at the Smurfs and swore at them as he went running off down the hill.

"You won't hear the last of this" he shouted. But all the Smurfs and the miller could do was laugh. The Smurfs were not afraid of Gargamel and they knew he would not put a curse on Frank's mill again.

From that day onwards, whenever the Smurfs took their grain to the mill, they received free flour.

CATCH A FISH

Answer: 3

Smurf Sunbathing

DOT TO DOT